23 June 1988

So Steven —

Dearest of dear
friends.
Let's soon lift a glass
to comfort, honesty,
understanding, and joy.
(I don't think we're
exactly sure about
"happiness" at every
juncture.)

Love —
Peg

(P. S. Ah yes — a little
"success" now and then
can't hurt . . . .)

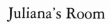

Juliana's Room

Juliana's Room

by Margaret Lally

Bits Press
Cleveland

The author thanks the Ohio Arts Council for an Individual
Artist's Fellowship, during which most of these poems were
written.

Published by Bits Press with the support of grants from
The Citadel and the Ohio Arts Council.

Art by Michael Gutzwiller. The figure on the cover is drawn
from the monumental sculpture of Coatlicue, Aztec goddess of
Earth and of Fertility. In spite of her horrific aspect, which
represents her power, she was regarded as a beneficent deity,
"mother of the four hundred Southern stars."

Printed in the U.S.A.

ISBN 0-933248-10-5

For Michael and Patrick,

whose good sense and love

are always shining

We only came to sleep,
We only came to dream.
It is not true, was never true
We came to live on earth.

I am only the grass of springtime.
Like all the others, my heart will grow green
And open its petals in silence.

All that stays bright is the sun.

— Aztec poem

. . . And if your minds are set upon me,
And ye remember me as a father, permit no man
to take my body and carry it into Egypt. . . .
Dig a grave then, and bury me therein, and hide
my body under the earth, and let these my words
be observed carefully by you, and tell ye no man
where ye lay me; and there shall I be until
the Resurrection of the dead, when I shall receive
again this body without corruption.

— Saint Anthony

Julia Pastrana (1832–1860) was a Mexican "digger" Indian, who was billed in sideshows and performances across Europe as "The Ugliest Woman in the World." Shaggy hair covered her stunted body, and her feet were hooflike. Her face bore the features of an ape; stiff black hair and crossed black eyes gave her a wild and sullen aspect. Her manager, a Mr. Lent, found it profitable to costume her in a gaudy red velvet dress and dancing shoes and to set her to dancing onstage. (Always, onstage or off, she wore about her neck a large silver crucifix.)

The shell of her ugliness contrasted sharply with the actuality of her mind and character. From all accounts, Julia Pastrana was brilliant, kind, soft-spoken, and spiritually elegant. Like all nineteenth-century "monsters," she was kept in a kind of social quarantine, lest she lose her shock value, but she used that time to read, and over the years she educated herself superbly in her isolation. Those few individuals who gained entrance to her room were astonished at the dissonance between what they saw and what they felt in her presence.

As the poem begins, Juliana is considering a change of managers, and Lent, an attractive man, has suddenly responded with a proposal of marriage. She is amazed at the offer. Others in the company attempt to warn her that he is only trying by the most desperate means to keep her from leaving him. She has become an extraordinarily valuable property, and has already brought him considerable wealth.

1852. Juliana's Mirror:

Beyond one curtain, the stir of rain,
Mutter of coaches' hooves,
The water and clatter of night.

Beyond the other, the stir of disgust,
Heyday of coins, patter and thunder of hands.

Juliana, stay here. Stay in your room.
Face the shining wall, and learn.
I never darken, never applaud, never lie.
I tell you only what is.
Go out when you must, then come home.
I give you truth, not beauty.

Tonight you will dance. Set your heart
And your little dark hooves into shoes;
Swing so fast your heart becomes blurred:
Swoop of scarlet, spinning rose,
Fingers' flick, sparrows' wings,
Trinketing castanets. Dance.

But you can't dance forever. The heart
Winds down, face comes clear:
And they see your monkey face, your riddled hide,
Shaggy breast. You can't be always dancing.

You're alone. Learn that. Forever.
Nothing you do will appease them:
They'll never care for the ivory cross,

The plea in the song, or the silk, or the ribbon.
You are a woman past flowers.

Look at me. I give you again
A wither of hair, terrier's jowl,
Leather nose, mane, beard,
Skull primordial.

Of course, you needn't look.
Put out the light.
Put out your eyes.

She Speaks to Him:

Mr. Lent. You call this a paw by day,
And now you choose to run your lips
Over my ragged hand by the light of the lamp.

God has cursed me with strong brown eyes.
All day I look at Amanda and Jane. Yes,
I see your eyes: they leap at their dance,
Like flames that leap at the grate.
I see all too well. This plague should have given me
Fullness of blight, or a tribe for the sharing.

Amandas and Janes, all natural and right, like
All the world's trees, that somehow never sprouted
Stone leaves; like a wilderness of dogs,
Trotting down streets: not one with the face of a bird.
Not like me. There is no confusion like me.

Look at me, Sir, before you kiss that hand.
Look at me: my dress is more like
To God's image and likeness than I am.
I keep that mirror fixed on my wall —
It reminds me that I'm Queen:
Queen of toads, of wombats, of fainting wives.
I know my place, Mr. Lent. This room.
I shall never leave.

I have taught myself. I shall not see God a long time —
Not in that mirror, and not in man's eyes.
I shall only see God when I cast off this skin,

And slither, like a bleeding snake, into His arms.
Like a child, for hours I will whisper wild questions.

Look closely, Sir. I keep a crucifix around my neck
To remind them: of Sunday songs,
And Nazareth, and Mary's many tears.
They know no one on earth would dare thread Jesus
About a monkey's neck. I put it there myself, Sir,
To declare that I am woman, not a thing.
Since they can't see my heart, I show them His.

Love Jesus, then, if you don't love yourself;
Take your hands away. Suffice it that I profit you.
Don't make me your toy.

I sleep with memories would curdle your brain.
And you're a fine man, with April in your skin,
And drifting weathers in your voice.

From the night of my birth,
My father slept in a corner alone.
He said Satan had taken his bed.
My mother crooked and bobbed her head like a crow,
And spoke only my father's name.
The villagers made the Sign whenever she passed.

When everyone slept,
An old woman took me up
And washed me in the river.

Shortly after Juliana left her native village, she wrote
these words to her mother. She gave the letter to
the village priest, and asked him to continue to carry
it to her mother, for as long as was necessary, until
she could comprehend her daughter's message.

My mother, I am told that still you whisper,
Still you talk to little dreams.

In your lasting quiet, do you wander the path of children,
Looking for one such as me?
Do you pass through the gates again and again
And climb down the crumbling stairs of time
Seeking a face like my own?

How deep you have traveled.
How far you have gone.

Do you move through the folds of the lives of our people
Toward the beginning of time?
Do you live now in legends the old men have told?
At the Hill of the Bird, the Place of the Song?

Do you come to the slope
Where the tombs face west, into the falling sun?

Do you see the red dogs of Colima
Carrying souls to the opposite bank of the river?
Do you see the rotting spiny god,
The Moan Bird aloft on his shoulder?
Or the Four who stand at the corners of earth,
Who hold up the sky with their hands?

Are you gone from Spanish men and Spanish days,
Wandering Mazatán, The House of Flowers,
Through Day of Wind, and Day of Water,

Day of House, and Day of Death,
Seeking a child like a beast?

Find the dolls, Mother.
Go far enough to find the old dolls:
The dwarfs, the hunchbacks, the twins, and
Two-headed, the three-eyed children who smiled —
Who lived by the god of all life and the morning.

In days when priests with eyes wild as mine
Climbed the temples' thousand stairs
Till the call of the macaws and monkeys went dim,
And trees knelt like dogs at their feet:

In those days the Maya knew
A family with bodies gone mad —
Their feet twisted roots;
Their jaws like the jaguar's;
Their hands of six fingers.
And they were the greatest of Maya:
Because they bred monsters, men called them divine.

Now, Father lives by scratching stones.
You whittle clots of air.

Find the dolls, Mother.
If you live in a garden of beautiful children,
Look to the little places in walls
For creatures like me.

You were not the wrong mother,
Nor I the wrong daughter.
It was the wrong time.

May Jesus and the gods of time
Take your life in their arms.

Juliana Writes in Her Journal:

They're wrong about Lent.

I try to brush past them, but still one or two find my ear:
"Think! He doesn't love you."
"He loves no one but himself."
"He has only coins trickling through his veins."

But I know. I know him now.
I've thrown every scorn in his way;
Still he's sought and found my hand.
His touch — it's mild as petals.
I've baited him, sniped at him,
Turned a cold back.
He only says, "Stay here with me.
Stay with me all your life."

Ah, the peace.
Evenings, he comes through the door —
We read Shakespeare.
The fire sings. I cover my brow
With my hands as I read, and, in a moment, I'm Juliet.
Or, for love of me, the Moor stays at the bedside,
Poised between lips and the tomb.
For me, Macduff can show them only little rags of grief.

I spend my time undoing the Creation:
I pray, "Let there be Darkness."

But, in the dark, he finds me.

He leads me to myself.

He takes me back, unties black memories, throws them
        away.
My mother's quaking shawl,

The cool hard swirl of the priest's frock,
Where I buried my face in fear of the others;
The stench and claws behind the market stall,
Where they locked me in and laughed at me all night.

He takes me away, in the darkness.
I leave behind the old black village,
The hot bleating tongues of the footlights.
In the dark, he finds me lovely.
He reaches out his two hands
And leads me out of hell.

He loves me.
For myself alone.

1858. Juliana Awaits the Birth of Her Child:

I'm not alone tonight.

I feel his bones roll slowly,
Like lolling clouds inside me.
I sit in this chair
And watch the fire.
With three fingertips, I trace
His elbow, or his knee. Sometimes, I think,
His tiny fingers press on mine.

How my frock moves.
Little bones bubble under flowers.
He starts a bit when a door slams.
He hears a song outside the glass.

And, inside his dark,
He smiles his father's smile.
All I love begins again:
I carry my love, and I carry a man
Of the twentieth century.
A chuckle, a voice,
A lean, tan hand to sign a name —
His name, my name — Lent.

I need only live.
Protect the heart under my heart.
Nature has granted me justice,
Given me all of the years to live over,
All for such a little bit of pain.

I'll have a new wardrobe, when I'm once again small:
All-colored veils, violets and mosses —

I'll smother my face in the whole month of May.
My veils will swirl under impudent hats.

And then we'll play games by the river:
We'll flit among trees, better than birds.
His father and I will show him the world,
    from phaetons and trains.
I'll teach him my languages, all of them.

And, in our home . . .
In our home, we'll have a chapel made to childhood.
He'll stand in his red velvet jacket on Christmas night,
    I'll sing centuries of songs.
Then I'll set him on the floor, cross-legged,

And hide behind screens. He'll roll backward
    with laughter. My puppets
    will run and steal wigs, and pinch snuff,
    and beat marching songs out on a spinet.

When my show is done,
    he'll muddy their faces with sweets,
    asking them if they are real.

In our home, every year,
    we'll have parties with masks;
    I'll paint them myself. I'll stand so high
    at the head of the stairs, with my arms
    full of masks. I'll call, "Faces for everyone.
    Come choose your own." I'll be Diana
    this New Year, Salome in June.
    I'll not be homely the first twenty years.

And, long after dark, we'll sit close near the wall.
I'll make puppies and rabbits from shadows.

After night prayers, I'll sing him lullabies
    that only the Indians know.

1859. Moscow. Juliana Gives Birth:

Harder. It comes harder.
    Hot   a devil's pulse

Child — no
    stones   hot silent stones

I want to stop   the devil everywhere
    I don't want this

Take it away
    give me back   my body

I'll run away   climb out
    leave the stones burning on each other

I'll go away   I'll sleep
    Lent?

1859. A Midwife:

At dawn I came into her room.
For an hour I couldn't touch her skin,
And I a midwife.

That poor struggling hide,
Those whispers, those eyes.

Toward evening I asked about Lent.
She said that he'd been strange of late,
    perhaps he'd gone to find a little gift.
And she turned her face to the wall.

Near midnight, it was quiet there;
I helped her with her pains.
May God forgive: Each time I saw that face,
I thought, "Who could call that 'Mother'?"

Then I heard stomping, shoes in the hall.
I heard laughter.

             And there stood Lent,
A cigar in his hand, a grin on his face.
And close behind him, men of every kind,
    bareheaded, in caps, in dirt,
A gang of men. They coughed and looked around.

They all went quiet, first.
But Lent, he hailed them in.

Oh, where was Nature then?

Even the housecat slips into the dark,
And returns in the morning,
With soft life squirming in her jaws.

And where was heaven then?
Where was an angel, to blow out the candles?
Someone to guard her, with his sword?

Or just some superstition would have done.
Someone to say, "This surely is unlucky, man.
Keep the money. I'll be on my way."

But no. Not one. Nothing intervened.
They stood. They ground their ashes on the floor.
They wagered on its sex, its shade of hair.

That night I handled her infant.
God should never have dressed it in blood,
        so great was the curse laid on it
        by birth, and by death.

1860. London. A Shopkeeper:

I hear she lost an infant, there in Russia —
An ape, just like herself. She died of grieving.

Well, who can say.
I'm sure I never know at all.
One hears every sort of lie about these monsters.
They're on the move,
Say what they please.
Most of it is rot.
It's done with mirrors.

Come to that, she's dead,
At twenty-eight.

Well, rest in peace.

She's quite like any other woman now.

Shortly after the deaths of Julia Pastrana and her baby son, Lent took both their bodies and presented them to be mummified. Before long, they were seen on exhibition. Her dark, hairy face now stared out from inside a glass box. Julia wore, as she had in life, her ornate red dress; her child was dressed in a red velvet suit. Her body stood upon a small table. His was erect upon a kind of perch, such as are used for birds.

I was handed over to the stench of Egypt,
    to a man in a hidden necropolis.

He drew out my brain through my nostril,
    tied my nails to my bones with thread,
    soaked this bag of skin for forty days.

He cut open my flank and reached deep inside,
    filled my head with swabs of cloth,
    left beads for my eyes,
    stoppered my neck with wax.

He tore out my intestines,
    but let my heart hang in its place.
He painted my flesh with resin.

In Cairo long ago they laid them down,
    and made of them what I am.
But they left them goods to help them on their way,
    and swaddled them in linen, and said prayers.

They laid them down, in Cairo.

Throughout the course of the nineteenth and twentieth centuries, the glass case containing Julia Pastrana and her child was sighted at sideshows and carnivals across Europe.

It is said that in 1972 the two bodies were on display in a sideshow in Jacksonville, Florida.

1972. Juliana:

Beggars' music rolls across the midway.
The hungry-eyed, the curious, ply their faith,
And horror says its prayers.

Even here I remember the rain.
That much I know.

Your faces never change.
You look like your fathers.

You stare at me,
You laugh with silver teeth.

You study my skin.
You finger my tomb.

The road and a thousand hands
Have almost killed me.
But through my marble eyes I see:
I see lights bursting at midnight.
I see wild colors fly past on wheels.

A swollen face sells beer:
I hear his voice.
Little papers flutter everywhere,
Splinters glint on cinders.

We two are red rag statues, molded mud.

I have stood in this dancing dress a hundred years,
    my young child beside me.
My hair hangs and frays like dusty rope.

My belly and loins sag
    with sawdust and sinking cloth.
My heart is dark and dry.

I have been sold to the Pharoahs.

I am not alone.

Someday the glass will smash,
    and the dust of my face will crumble.

What was done to me was done also to my son.

An iron bar first stood him on his feet.

Each night I see his bones shift ever so little.
His eye is slipping down.

Oh, Lent.
You should have let the baby sleep.

In ancient Egypt it was believed that the Ba, *the soul and manifestation of the one dead, could leave its body by day and assume any shape it chose. At sunrise, it rose up everywhere from the enormous rooms where the mummified bodies lay together. It flew across earth with the others, and continued on its own way. Wherever it came to rest, it could invade any living form it desired.*

The Ba *is usually portrayed and visualized as a bird with a human head.*

Juliana. At Dawn:

You —
      you are my lasting breath,
      knit with the wind.
      Rise up from my womb in a whisper,
      rise up from my womb toward the sun —
      when sunlight chimes, climb out of our bones
          to fly into daylight waves,
            to call to our brothers in tears

Soar over mountains,
plunge through the silence,
drift through the dim rifts of light

Then find the land, and find the body;
      slip down the channel of some quiet throat;
      nest under flesh in the sun

Stand in the grey wells of shadow.
      Stand, near the Russian church.
      Stand, and wait, and stand, and whisper:
      Wait, all day in the shadows

With darkness, climb into my eyes again

Mr. Lent, after the deaths of his wife and son, discovered another monstrous, isolated young woman. He courted and wed her, thereafter introducing her to audiences across the continent as the sister of Julia Pastrana.

But in time he began to behave in bizarre ways. In Russia, in the last phase of his life, he was seen standing alone on a bridge, talking, and tearing up bank notes that he threw into the river Neva.

He died of brain disease in 1884.

Margaret Lally holds a Ph.D. in modern British and American literature; her research interests are D. H. Lawrence and W. B. Yeats.

Her two grown sons live in Ohio. She lives in Charleston, South Carolina, where she teaches the writing of fiction and poetry at The Citadel.